MY BOW-ARM METHOD

For

Violin

Based on Open Strings Exercises

Intermediate-Advance
Volume I

©2013
By Rafael M. Ramirez, DMA

Introduction

MY VIOLIN BOW-ARM METHOD establishes a logical sequence of exercises, giving the violin student and teacher a sequential lesson plan to address bow technique. Each exercise is targeted to achieve mastery of a specific technical element of bowing. Exercises' difficulty increases progressively to ensure proficiency in all elements of violin bow technique.

The most important objective of this method is to assist the violin player to prepare for an everyday practice session. The method will help to develop bow control.

These exercises must be done in all strings for better results.

TABLE OF CONTENTS

ELEMENTARY RUDIMENTS

It is important to know the basics before playing the violin. This chapter will help the student to understand the fundamental elements of the violin such as: parts of the violin, parts of the bow, basic music theory, and more.

Parts of The Violin

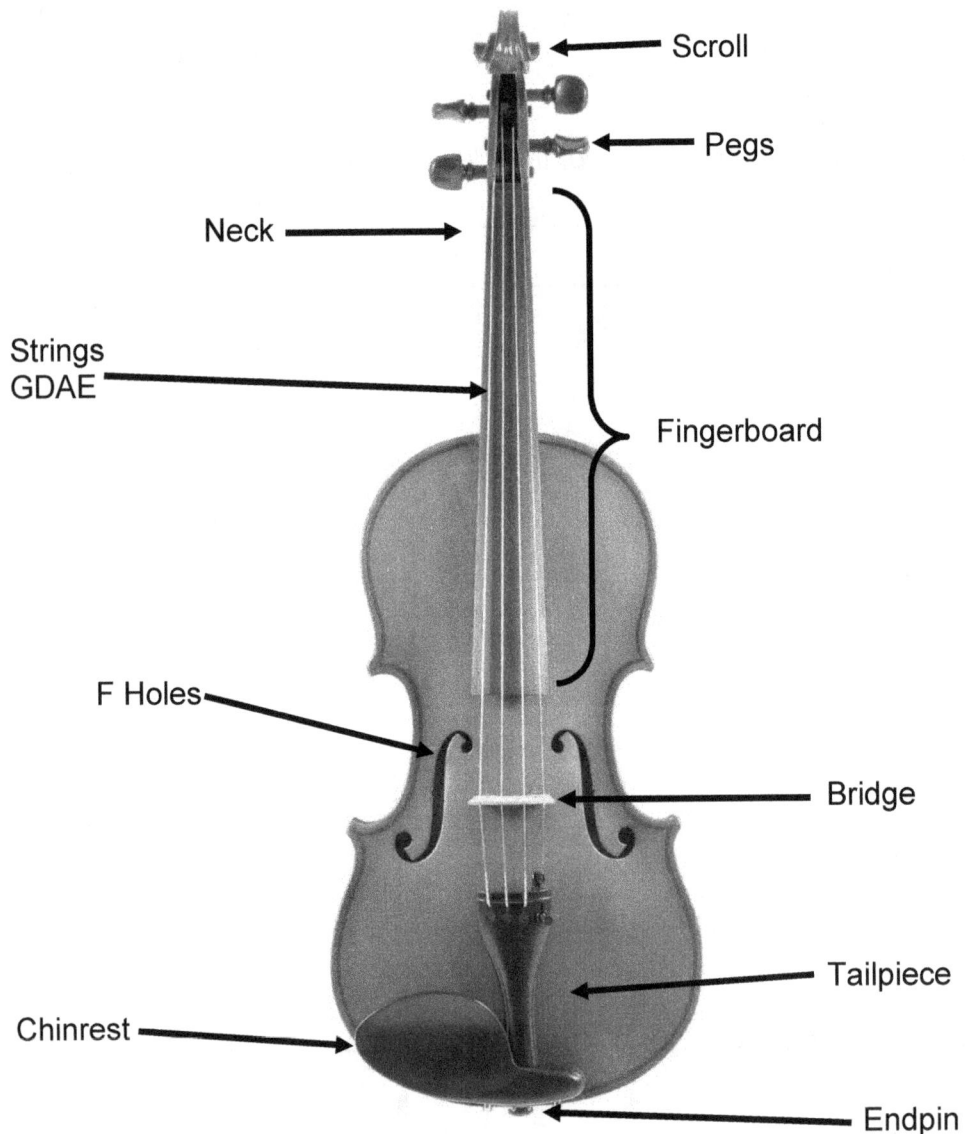

Parts of the Bow

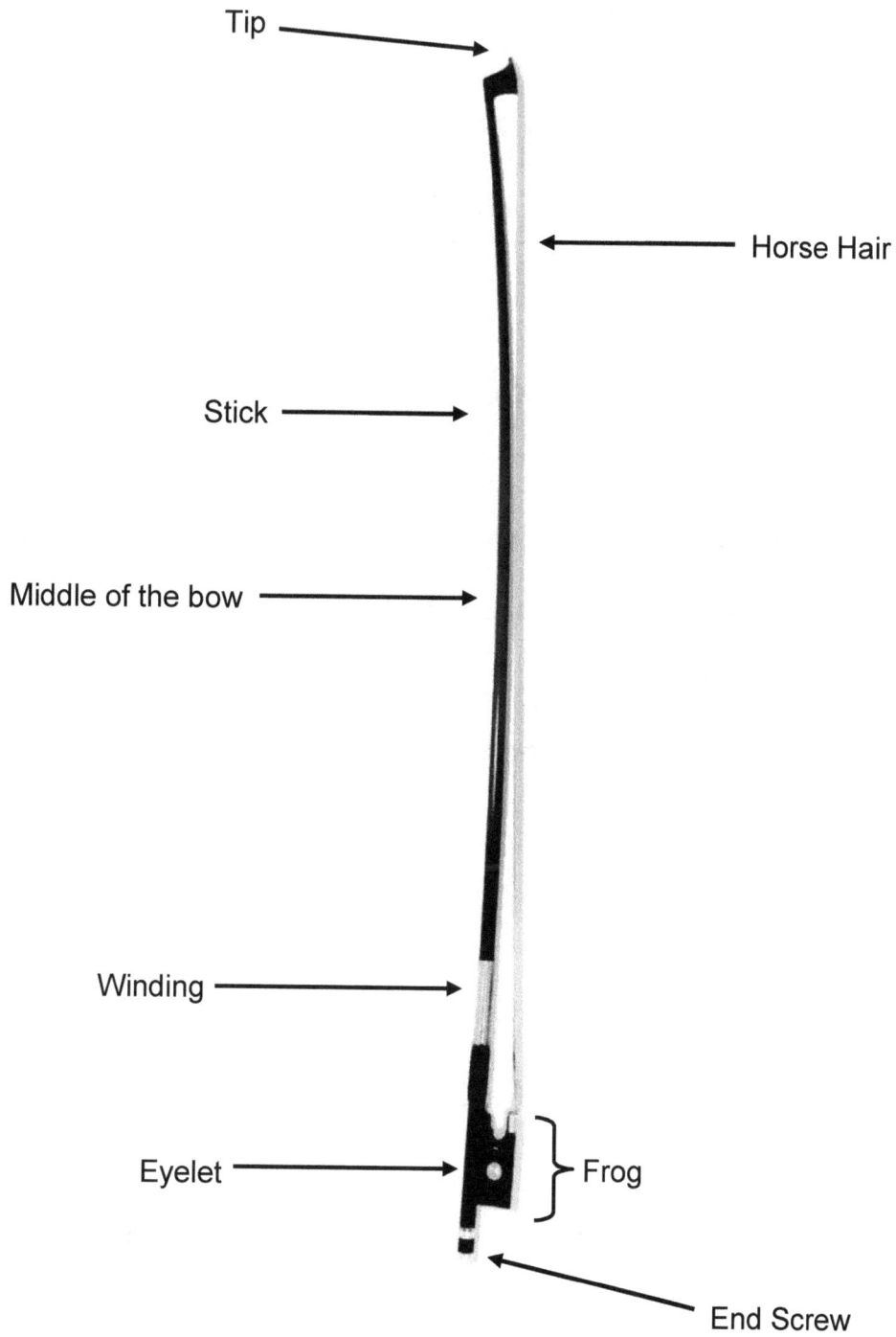

Tip

Horse Hair

Stick

Middle of the bow

Winding

Eyelet

Frog

End Screw

An Introduction to Music Theory

Pitches

C	D	E	F	G	A	B
Do	Re	Mi	Fa	Sol	La	Si

The Music Staff

The music staff (the pentagram) is used to notate music. It has 5 lines and 4 spaces. Each one of the lines and spaces represents a pitch. The name is given to each line and space depending on the clef.

The Staff

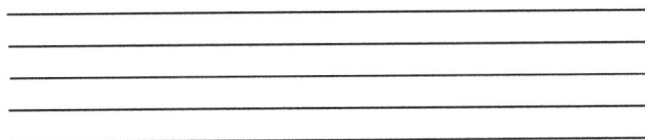

The Clef

Music for violin is written in treble clef. The clef indicates the position of the notes in the music staff and gives each line and space a particular name. We can find the clef at the beginning of the music staff.

The Treble Clef (G-clef)

The treble clef for the violin is placed in the second line (going up) of the music staff. Because the circle of the g-clef is on this line, the line will be named G. When a note is on this line, it will have the same name as the line, which is G.

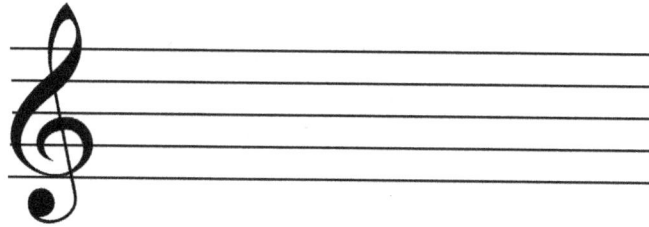

Names of the Lines and Spaces of the Music Staff

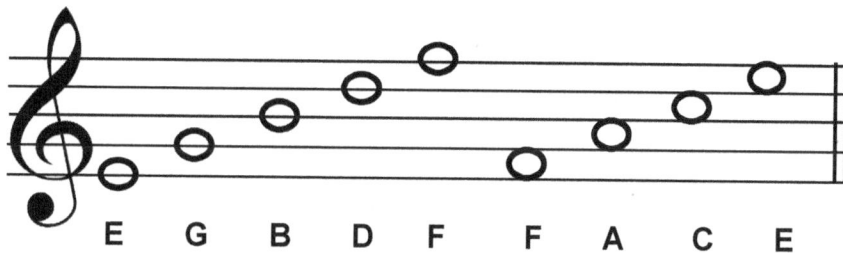

E   G   B   D   F   F   A   C   E

For all the exercises presented in this book, we are going to be using four notes only: G, D, A, and E, which correspond to the open strings of the violin.

Open Strings of The Violin

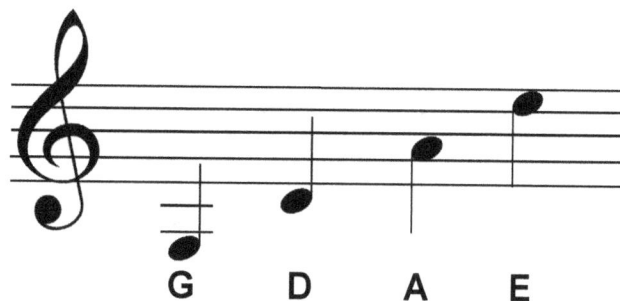

G   D   A   E

The Beat

The beat is the basic unit of time.

Note Duration

Musical notation indicates the duration of a sound. When we know the duration of a note, we will be able to perform music with precision. Also, depending on location of the note on the music staff, pitch will be different.

In this method, we will be using the following note value:

Symbol	Name	Value
o	whole note	4 beats
♩	half note	2 beats
♩	quarter note	1 beat
♪	eighth note	1/2 beat
♪	sixteenth note	1/4 beat

Parts of the Note

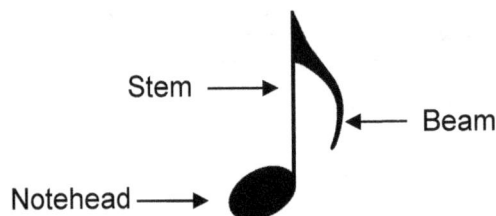

Stem ⟶

⟵ Beam

Notehead ⟶

Rests

In order to make music we need silence; silence is important, so we can hear and organize rhythm. When we place notes and rests together we can make different types of rhythms. We will be using in this method the following rests:

Symbol	Name	Value
▬	whole rest	4 beats
▬	half rest	2 beats
𝄽	quarter rest	1 beat
𝄾	eighth rest	1/2 beat
𝄿	sixteenth rest	1/4 beat

Time Signatures

The time signature tells us how many beats are in one measure (the top number) and what type of note represents one beat in the measure (the bottom number). We can find the time signature at the beginning of a piece, and in our case it will be at the beginning of each exercise. We are going to use only the simplest time signatures, seen below:

$$\frac{2}{4} \qquad \frac{3}{4} \qquad \frac{4}{4}$$

The Repeat Bar

The repeat bar tells us that we need to repeat a specific music passage.

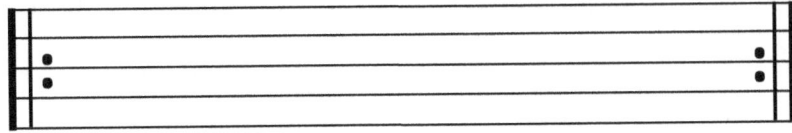

Dynamics

Dynamics tell us how loud or soft the music should be played. We will use the following symbols:

Symbol	Name	Meaning
F	Forte	Loud
P	Piano	Soft
<	Crescendo	Gradually increasing volume
>	Decrescendo or diminuendo	Gradually decreasing volume

Rhythm

Rhythm is the placement of sound in time; we use accents, meters, and tempos as elements to organize sound and silence.

Bow Direction

We will use the symbols in this table to indicate bow direction.

Symbol	Name	Meaning
⊓	down bow	bow travels in the direction of the floor
V	up bow	bow travels in the direction of the ceiling

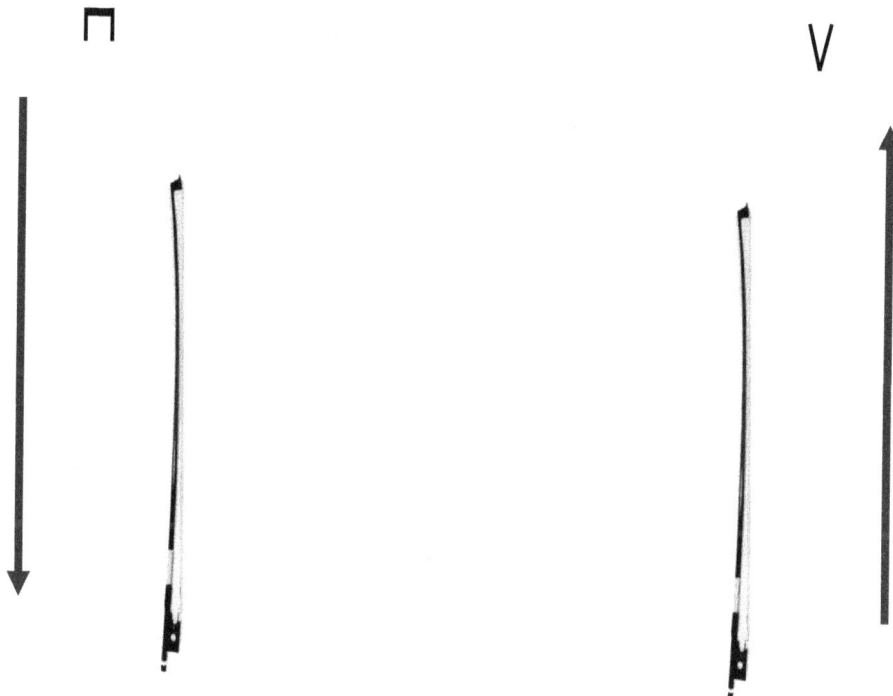

⊓

V

Bow Arm Exercises (Open Strings)
Single String Exercises

Directions:

- Use whole bow (W.B.).
- Always start on string.
- Contact point.
- Flat hair.

- Consistent bow speed.
- Practice this exercise at various tempos (largo, Adagio, Andante, Allegro, Presto).
- Practice using following crescendo and decrescendo patterns:

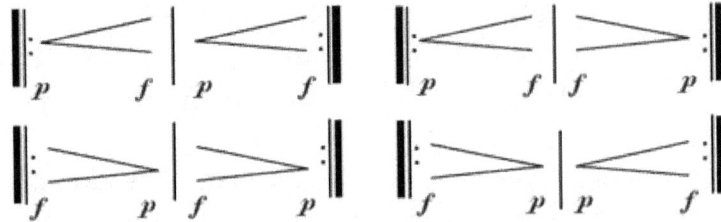

Exercise # 1 (o: whole note)

R. Ramirez

Connect all notes - Practice using the following dynamics: FF, F, mf, mp, p, pp.

1.A. Whole notes, bow direction combination

Directions:

- To be performed with dynamics: F, p, FF, pp, mp, mf
- Practice using the crescendo and decrescendo patterns from Exercise 1
- Practice adding an accent > at the beginning of each note
- Bow speed must remain the same whether V or Π throughout the whole note
- Keep dynamics consistent for each note, connect each note to the other
- Contact point, play with flat hair
- Check fingers and posture

R. Ramirez

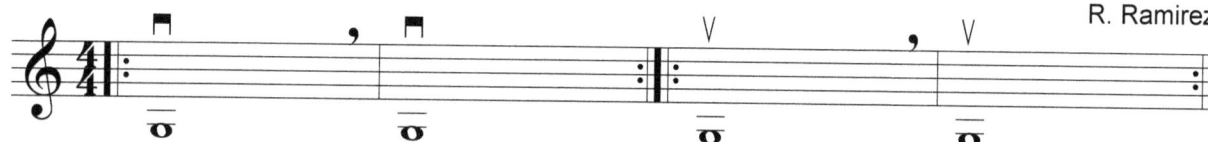

1.B. Whole note and half note combination (to be practice on each string G, D, A, E)

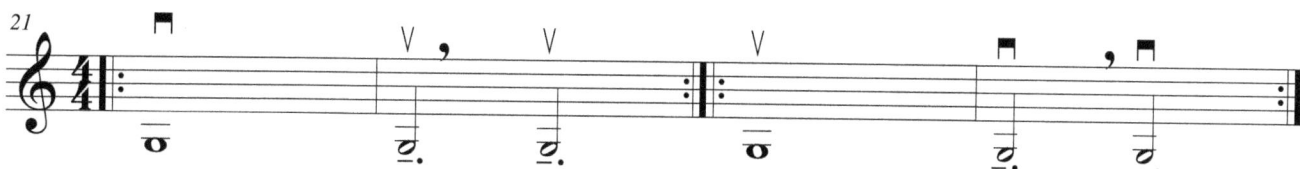

Exercise #2. ♩: The half note

Directions:
- To be performed with dynamics: F, p, FF, pp, mp, mf.
- Practice using the crescendo and decrescendo patterns from Exercise 1.
- Practice adding an accent > at the beginning of each note.
- Bow speed must remain the same whether V or ⊓ throughout the whole note.
- Keep dynamics consistent for each note, connect each note to the other.
- Contact point, play with flat hair.
- Check fingers on the bow and general posture.
- Practice this exercise at various tempos.

Practice playing Ex. 2 from:

- Frog to middle bow
- Middle bow to tip
- On the middle of the bow

R. Ramirez

Connect all notes

Exercise 2A. Half note Bow Direction Combination.

Directions:

- Practice on each string G, D, A, E.
- When two or more notes are to be played in succession with same
bow direction (such as Π Π or V V V). Retake the bow; also can be detaché Π' Π' Π' etc.

Practice playing from:

- Frog to middle bow
- Middle bow to tip
- On the middle of the bow

R. Ramirez

1. ‿·
2. Retake

Exercise #3.   ♩ : The Quarter Note

R. Ramirez

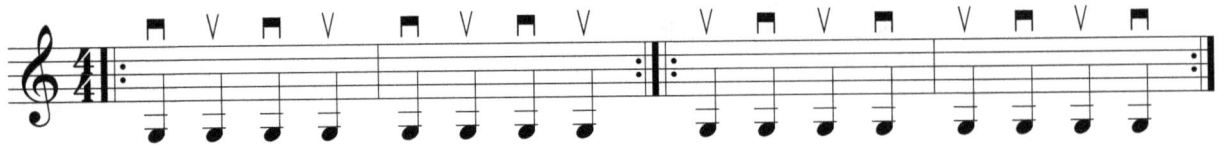

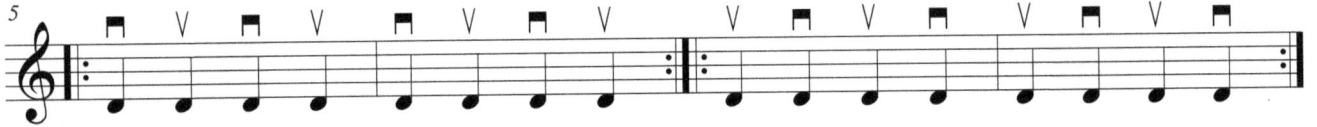

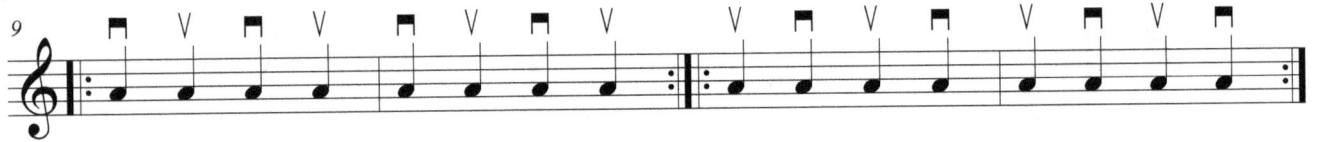

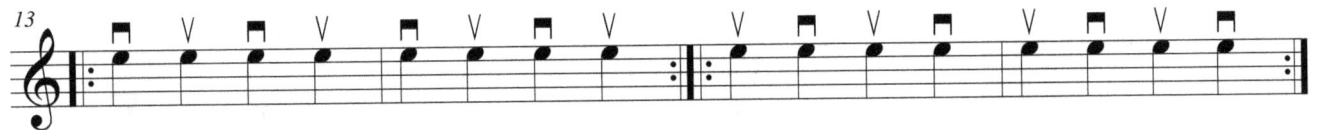

3A.* Connect all notes

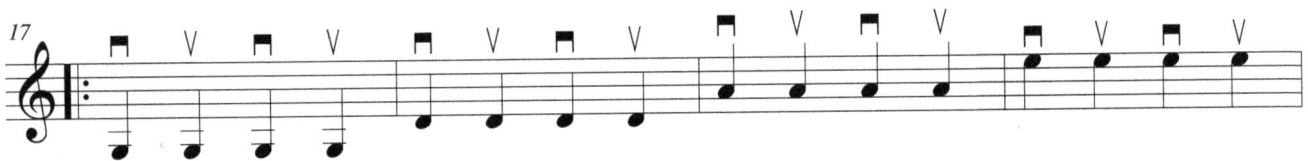

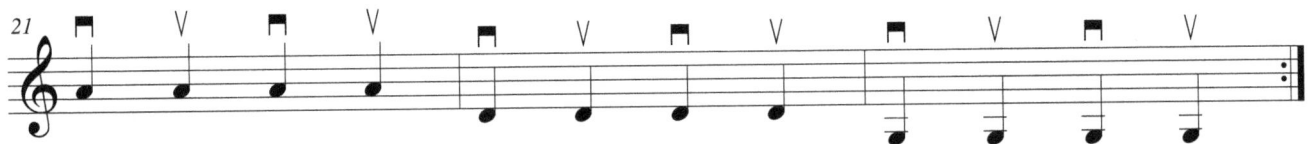

3B.*

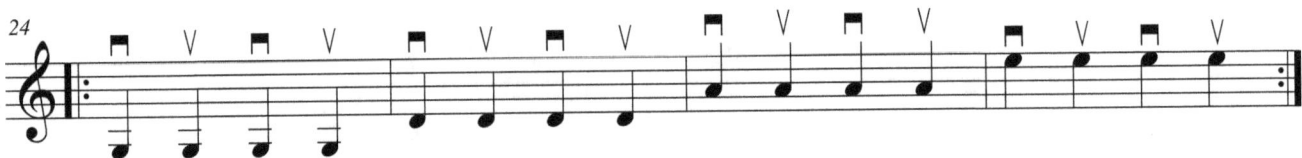

*Exercises 3A and 3B are also to be practiced using only ⊓ and V

Exercise 3C. The Quarter Note - Bow Changes

(To be practiced on each string G, D, A, E)

Directions:

Ex. 3C to be practiced using:

- Middle of bow, at the frog, at the tip, whole bow
- On the string at all time

- Legato stroke, detaché stroke
- Start on the string

R.Ramirez

Also practice Exercise 3C using the following accent patterns:

Exercise 3D. The Quarter Note and Quarter Rest

(To be practiced on each string G, D, A, E)

Directions:

- Practice using various dynamic level.
- Start on the string.
- Contact point.
- Flat hair.
- Maintain Same bow speed for each note group.
- Begin slowly and gradually work towards a faster tempo.

R. Ramirez

Exercise 4. ♪: The Eighth Note

(To be practiced on each string G, D, A, E)

R. Ramirez

Exercise 5. The eighth note and eighth rest

R. Ramirez

Exercise 6. ♩ & ♪ Combinations

Directions:

- Use whole bow (W.B.).
- Always start on string.
- Contact point.
- Flat hair.
- Consistent bow speed.
- Practice this exercise at various temp (Largo, Adagio, Andante, Allegro, Presto).

R. Ramirez

Exercise 7. ♩ & ♪ Triplet Combinations

R. Ramirez

Exercise 8. Quarter and Sixteenth Note Combinations

R. Ramirez

8A.

8B. **8C.**

Exercise 9. Eighth, Sixteenth, and Quarter Note Combinations

9A.

9B. **9C.**

9D. **9E.**

9F. **9G.**

Exercise 10. Half, Quarter, and Eighth Note Combinations

R. Ramirez

10A.

10B. **10C.**

10D. **10E.**

Exercise 11. Half Note, Quarter Note, Eighth Note, and Eighth Note Triplet Combination

11A.

11B. **11C.**

11D. **11E.**

11F. **11G.**

Exercise 12. Eighth, Sixteenth, Quarter, and Half Note Combinations

R. Ramirez

Exercise 13. Dotted Note Combinations

R. Ramirez

Two String Crossing Exercises

Directions:

- Practice on all strings (2 at a time) G-D, D-A, A-E.
- Play on the string
- Connected bow
- Legato
- Use varying dynamics F, p, FF, pp), and with crescendo and decrescendo patterns.

R. Ramirez

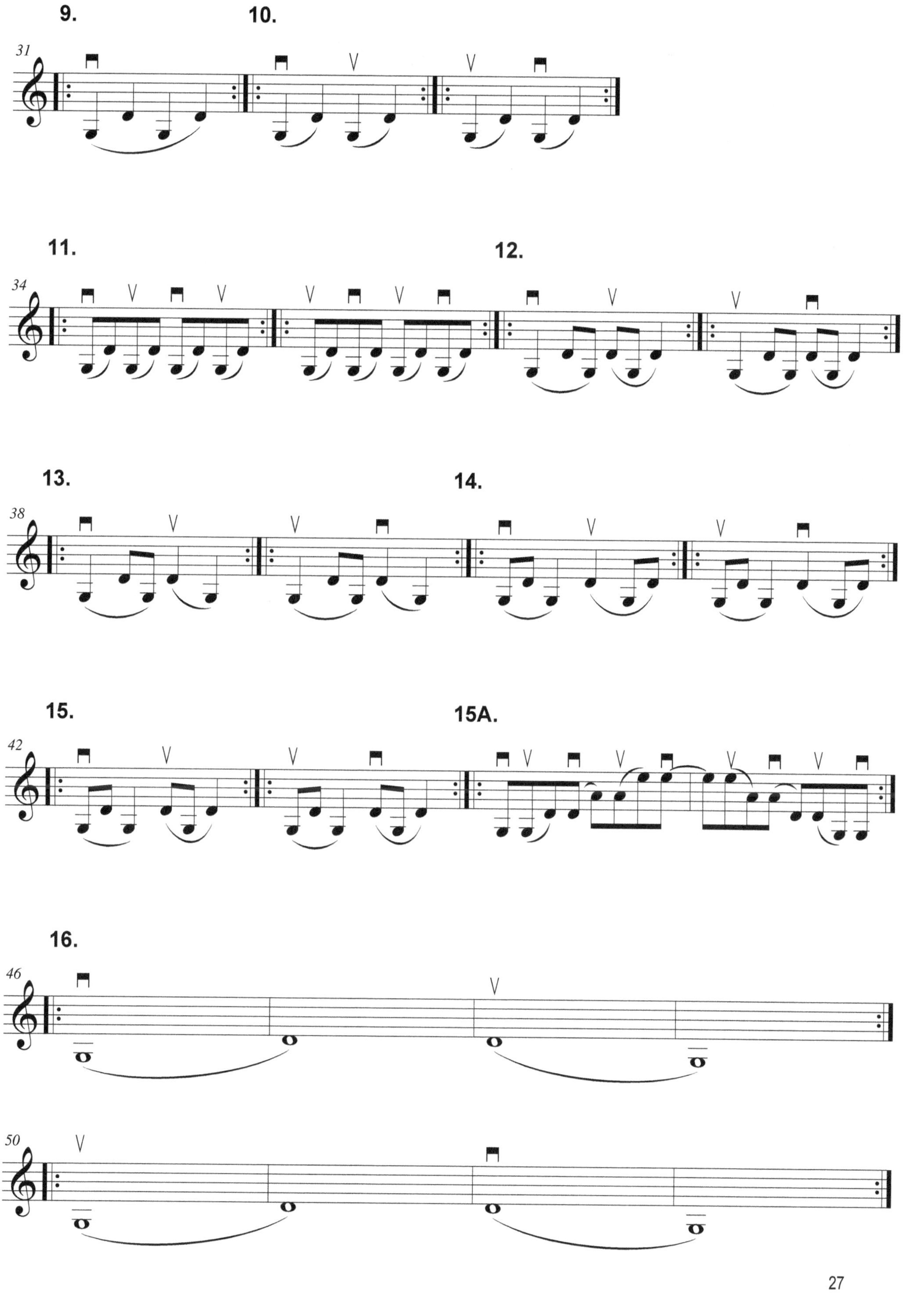
9.
10.
31
11.
12.
34
13.
14.
38
15.
15A.
42
16.
46
50

"The Wave" Exercise

Directions:

- To be practiced with, 𝅝, 𝅗𝅥, 𝅘𝅥 & 𝅘𝅥𝅮
- Practice only two strings at a time (G-D, D-A, A-E)
- Practice using various dynamic level.

Three String Crossing Exercises

Directions:
- Practice with 3 string combinations (3 at a time) G-D-A, D-A-E

R. Ramirez

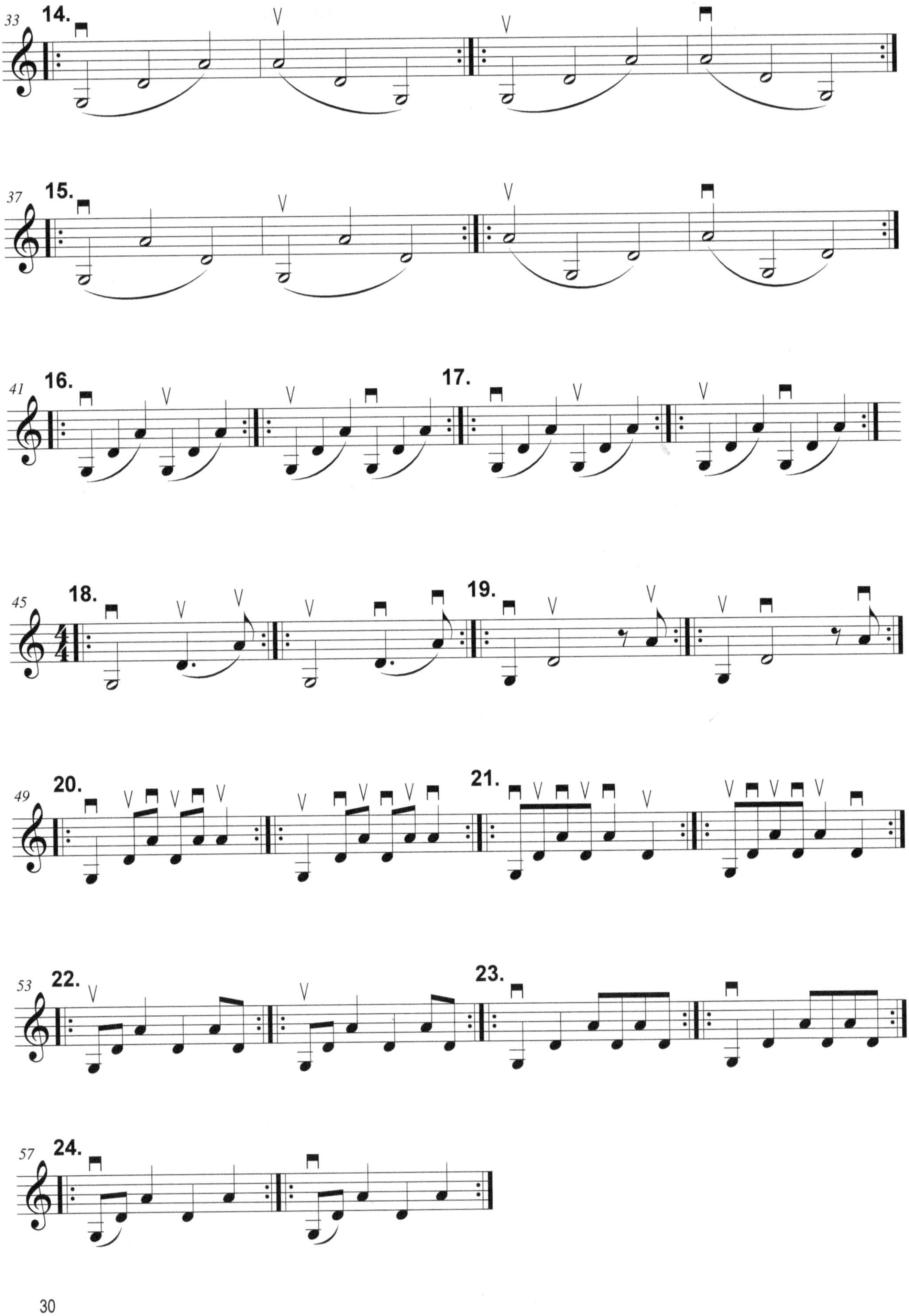
33
14.
37
15.
41
16.
17.
45
18.
19.
49
20.
21.
53
22.
23.
57
24.

25. **25A.**

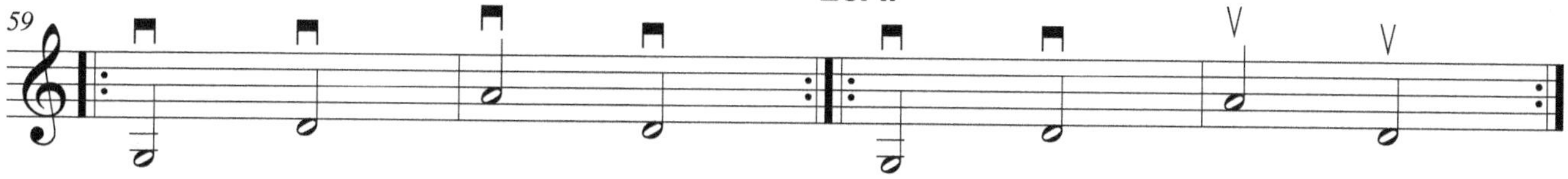

25B. **25C.**

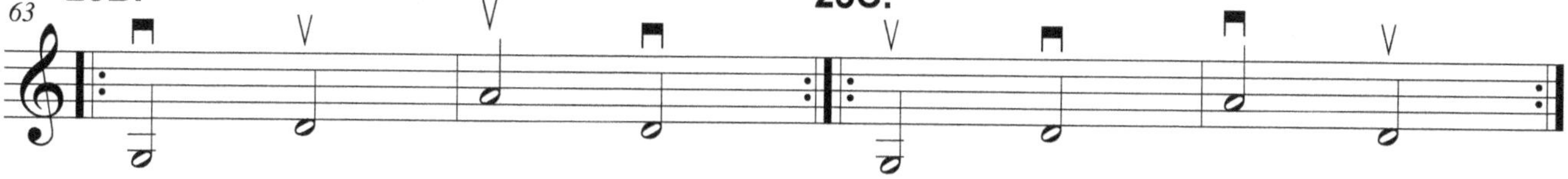

26.

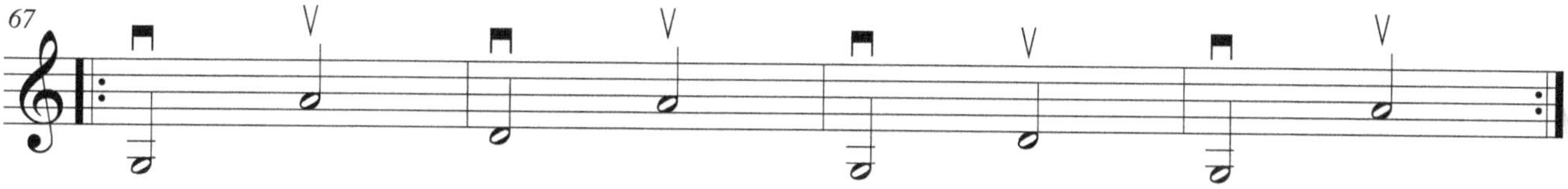

26A.

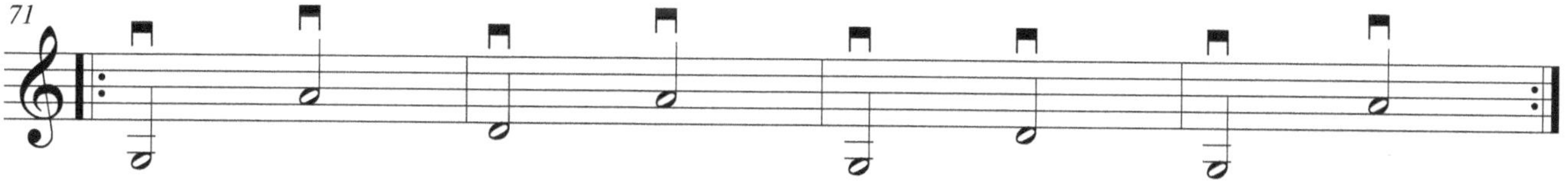

26B.

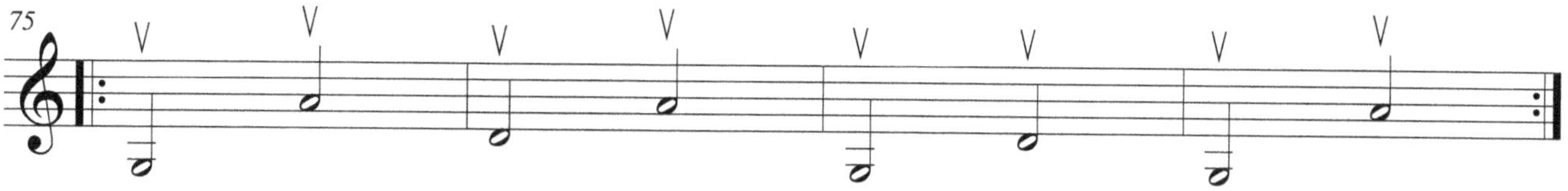

Four String Crossing Exercises

Directions:

- First play through the exercise using a legato stroke
then play through using martelé, staccato, and marcato.

- Practice at the frog, middle, and tip
- Also practice using varying dynamics and tempos.

R. Ramirez

10. **11.**

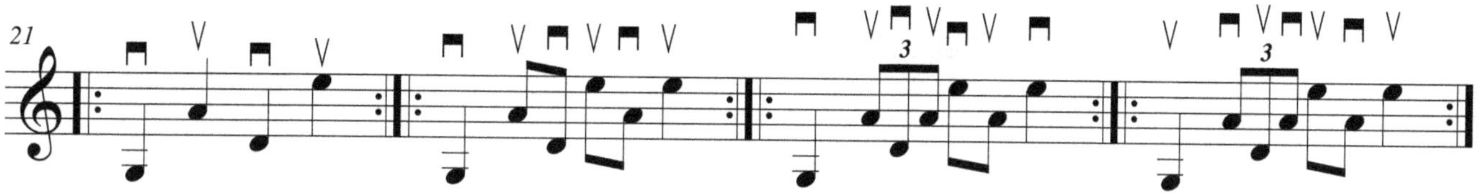

12.

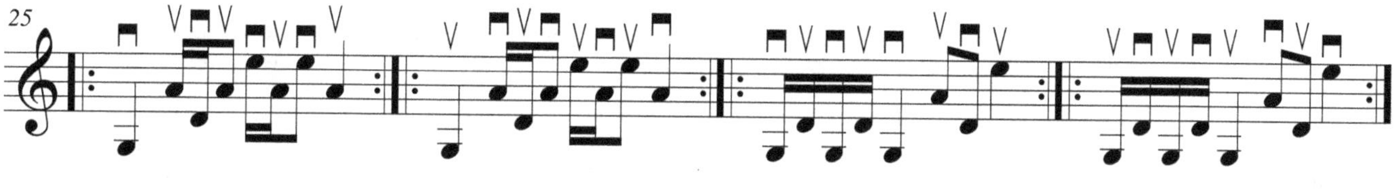

13.

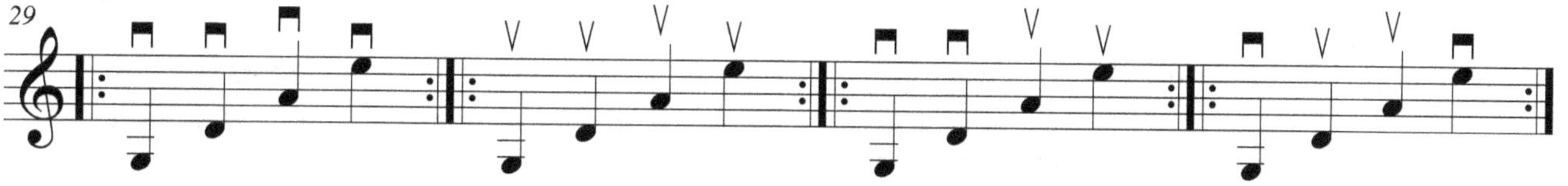

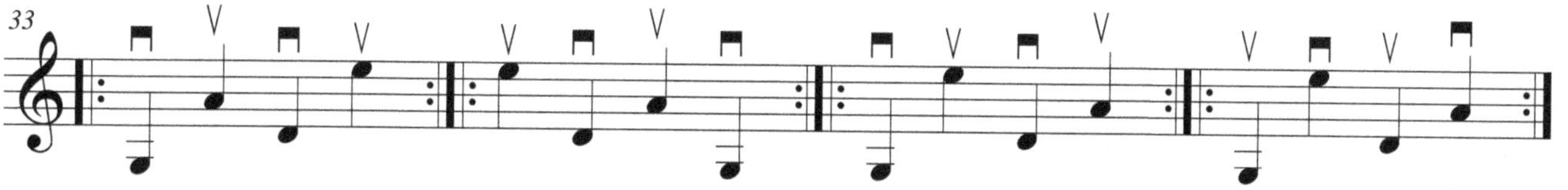

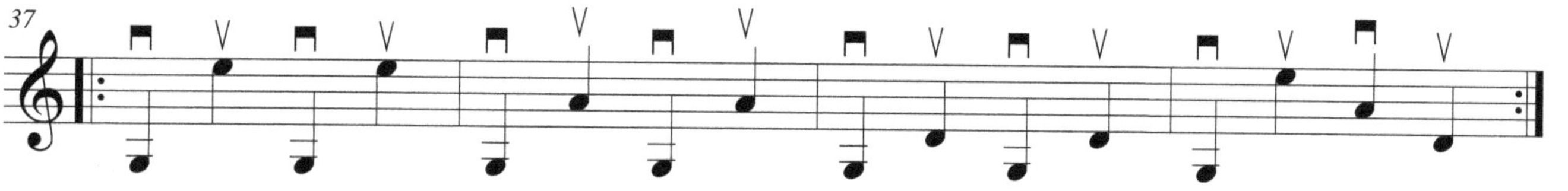

Four String Crossing Exercises

Practice on all string combinations G-D, D-A, A-E

R. Ramirez

20.

21.

22.

Practice to develop control on the tip and frog of the bow, to be practiced on all the strings (G-D, D-A, A-E)

frog   tip   tip   frog   frog tip frog tip   tip frog tip frog

frog   tip   tip   frog   frog   tip   frog tip frog tip

frog tip frog tip   tip frog tip frog

W.B

My Bow-Arm Method for Violin
Based on Open Strings Exercises
Intermediate-Advanced. Volume I (First Edition)

Credits
Author: Rafael M. Ramírez O., DMA
Editor: María A. Bermúdez, MS.
Cover Designer: Norman Bermúdez M.
Illustrator: Rafael M. Ramírez O., DMA
Prepared for Publishing by: María A. Bermúdez, MS.

Contact us at:
Email: rafaelramirezviola@gmail.com
Follow us:
Facebook: https://www.facebook.com/MusicEduTools/
Twitter: @rafaelramusic
Instagram: Music_Educational_Tools

www.ingramcontent.com/pod-product-compliance
Lightning Source LLC
Chambersburg PA
CBHW081154040426
42445CB00015B/1886